W9-AFV-827

This book is dedicated to
my friend Paul Dawson with
thanks for taking such good
care of me when Mummy
needed to work.

Love Finse

THIS BOOK
BELONGS TO

_____

_____

"Finse Explores France"

The right of Karine Hagen to be identified as the author
and Suzy-Jane Tanner to be identified as the illustrator
of this work has been asserted by them in accordance
with the Copyright Designs and Patents Act 1988.

First published by Viking Cruises
83 Wimbledon Park Side, London, SW19 5LP

Second edition published in 2015 by Viking Cruises.

ISBN 978-1-909968-05-9

www.finse.me

Produced by Colophon Digital Projects Ltd,
Old Isleworth, TW7 6RJ, United Kingdom
Printed in China.

FINSE
EXPLORES FRANCE

Karine Hagen
Suzy-Jane Tanner

Normandy Beaches

Rouen

Bayeux

Paris

Giverny

FRANCE

River Seine

River Loire

Chenonceau

N

Sarlat

Bordeaux

River Dordogne

River Garonne

2

Épernay

Lyon

River Rhône

Avignon

Arles

FINSE
EXPLORES
FRANCE

ITALY

Monte Carlo

I remember Grandpup telling me about our brave Collie Cross cousins who parachuted into France for the Normandy landings on D-Day in 1944.

Some paradogs were even honoured with the Dickin Medal for Gallantry.

I decided to visit Normandy and to explore France.

The Bayeux Tapestry is a huge embroidery telling the story of the Norman conquest of England in 1066.

It is said that Queen Matilda created it with her handmaidens.

It is 230 feet long and 20 inches wide!

Then I sailed to Rouen.
In 841 this was the Viking
capital in France and the
Norse leader Rollo was
made the first Duke of
Normandy.

The great cathedral even
has Viking rune inscriptions
to prove it.

ROLLO

I visited Claude Monet's house and wonderful garden at Giverny with its beautiful rose arches, bridges and ponds.

Monet painted many large Impressionist pictures of waterlilies and more.

I imagined watching him working in the garden.

11

The River Seine flows
through Paris, the capital
of France.

I went to the top of the
Eiffel Tower. Then I
visited many magnificent
museums and art galleries.

Fuddlewuddle and I
enjoyed shopping along
the wide boulevards too!

I visited Épernay, where they make the finest champagne.

This was first created accidentally when the bubbles made the corks pop in a cellar.

It is very expensive, so we only drink it on special occasions.

The Jacquard loom using punched cards to weave patterned silk was invented in Lyon.

The city is also the gourmet capital of France.

There are more than 365 French cheeses. My friend Didier Bouledogue showed me how to choose the best!

In 1669, flood waters swept away all but four arches of Avignon's old bridge.

I remembered the French nursery song and danced sur le pont!

Sur le Pont d'Avignon
On y danse, On y danse
Sur le Pont d'Avignon
On y danse tous en rond.

On the bridge of Avignon
We all dance there, we all dance there
On the bridge of Avignon
We all dance there, round and round.

Fuddlewuddle and I
sunbathed on the beach
at Monte Carlo, capital
of the principality of
Monaco.

We visited the beautiful
gardens outside the
Casino and met some
very rich and famous dogs.

Très chic!

21

The River Rhône runs into the Mediterranean near Arles, which was the most important Roman city in France.

The artist Vincent Van Gogh lived here. He painted sunflowers and starry night skies.

Fuddlewuddle and I visited the café where he used to paint.

In Sarlat I learned how to hunt for truffles from Farrah, the world famous trufficulteur.

Truffles grow under oak trees. They used to be found by pigs, but they ate them so dogs are better!

They are very costly, delicious and are used in the finest French dishes.

Bordeaux is a historic port,
famous for shipping wine
all over the world.

I travelled through nearby
vineyards and helped with
the harvest.

Grapes are traditionally
pressed by treading on them.
We had to wash our
paws first!

There are many elegant chateaux along the Loire river. I visited one at Chambord and then Chenonceau.

Many have beautiful formal flower gardens with statues and fountains.

I enjoyed meeting the gardeners, who were planting out their summer display.

The vegetables are grown
in elegant formal parterre
gardens too.

They reminded me of the
beautiful kitchen garden
at my puppyhood home,
Highclere Castle.

Goodbye France!
Au revoir France!

DOGOLOGY

Finse met her friends Farrah, Didier and many other fine French dogs on her journey.